# Marguerite,
## Go Wash Your Feet

Marguerite, go wash your feet,
The Board of Health's across the street.

# Marguerite,
## Go Wash Your Feet

**Wallace Tripp**

**HOUGHTON MIFFLIN COMPANY**

**BOSTON 1985**

*Library of Congress Cataloging in Publication Data*

Tripp, Wallace,
    Marguerite, go wash your feet.

    Summary: A collection of amusing verses by a variety
of poets, including Emily Dickinson, Spike Milligan,
Shakespeare, and other less well known.
    1. Children's poetry, English. 2. Children's poetry,
American. [1. Humorous poetry. 2. English poetry—
Collections. 3. American poetry—Collections] I. Title.
PR1175.3.T75   1985        821'.008'09282        85-7616
ISBN 0-395-35392-0

Printed in the United States of America
H 10 9 8 7 6 5 4 3 2 1

The author is grateful for permission to reprint the following poems:

"The Groaning Board," by Pink, from *Innocent Merriment*, by
    Franklin P. Adams. By permission of the Estates of Franklin
    P. Adams and Esther Root Adams.

"Teeth" and "Goliath," by Spike Milligan. By permission of Spike
    Milligan Productions Ltd.

"Epitaph on an Unfortunate Artist," by Robert Graves.

"On the Vanity of Earthly Greatness" and "Routine," from *Gaily the
    Troubadour,* by Arthur Guiterman; copyright © 1936. Reprinted
    by permission of Louise H. Sclove.

"We Had a Dog His Name Was Davey," by Sarah Ehrlich.

"Request Number," by G. N. Sprod; copyright © 1951 by
    Punch/Rothco. All rights reserved.

"The Texan was mighty hungry," "Rickenbacker," and "A dog is
    a pal," © by L.C. Briggs.

"Who are they who rudely jeer," To give advice I hesitate," and
    "Noah," © by R. Beasley.

"I saw a great scholar," © by Maude Crint.

If ever you go to Dolgelly,
Don't stay at the ——— Hotel;
There's nothing to put in your belly,
And no one answers the bell.

*Thomas Hughes*

7

## ROUTINE

No matter what we are and who,
Some duties everyone must do:

A Poet puts aside his wreath
To wash his face and brush his teeth,

And even Earls
Must comb their curls,

And even Kings
Have underthings.

*Arthur Guiterman*

I never forget a face—
But I am willing to make an exception in your case.

*Groucho Marx*

When Noah loaded the ark as bidden,
A few wily creatures stayed well hidden.
And that is why you never will see
The Vooner, the Sploke or the Gabbidee.

*R. Beasley*

To give advice I hesitate,
I never interpose.
You'll never see me dominate,
Or step on others' toes.
Thus I trust I'll not seem rude
If I by hints remind you:

There is a bear in search of food
About three feet behind you.

R. Beasley

Exit. followed by a bear.

There was a young bugler named Breen
Whose musical sense was not keen.
He said, "Ain't it odd.
I can never tell *God
Save the Weasel* from *Pop Goes the Queen*."

THAT'S MIGHTY PRETTY MUSIC. SOLDIER, GO ASK HIM
WHAT HE'S PLAYING.

HE SAYS IT'S A VIOLIN, SIR.

When I sat next to the Duchess at tea,
It was just as I feared it would be,
Her rumblings abdominal
Were something phenomenal—
And everyone thought it was me.

There was a young man so benighted,
He never knew when he was slighted.
   He went to a party,
   And ate just as hearty
As if he'd been really invited.

Rickenbacker flew a Spad Thirteen,
His hand was quick and his eye was keen.
He'd climb up high and wait in the sun,
Then drop like a hawk on the tail of a Hun,
Who recalled too late at the bullet's CRACK!
You never, never let Rick in back.

*L. C. Briggs*

Five little rabbits went out to walk;
They liked to boast as well as talk.
The first one said, "I hear a gun!"
The second one said, "I will not run!"
Two little ones said, "Let's sit here
        in the shade."
The big one said, "I'm not afraid!"
Bang, bang! went a gun,
And the five little rabbits run.

The time is out of joint: O cursed spite,
That ever I was born to set it right!

*William Shakespeare*

There's a wonderful family called Stein,
There's Gert and there's Ep and there's Ein;
  Gert's poems are bunk,
  Ep's statues are junk,
And no one can understand Ein.

A kind and gentle heart he had,
  To comfort friends and foes;
The naked every day he clad
  When he put on his clothes.

*Oliver Goldsmith*

Conductor, when you receive a fare,
Punch in the presence of the passenjare.
A blue trip slip for an eight-cent fare,
A buff trip slip for a six-cent fare,
A pink trip slip for a three-cent fare,
Punch in the presence of the passenjare!

Punch, brothers, punch with care!
Punch in the presence of the passenjare.

*Noah Brooks*

I'm glad the sky is painted blue;
    And the earth is painted green;
And such a lot of nice fresh air
    All sandwiched in between.

Great, wide, beautiful, wonderful World,
With the wonderful water round you curled,
And the wonderful grass upon your breast—
World, you are beautifully drest.

*William Brighty Rands*

19

When things were as fine as could possibly be
I thought 'twas the spring; but also it was she.

*John Byrom*

## ON THE VANITY OF EARTHLY GREATNESS

The tusks that clashed in mighty brawls
Of mastodons, are billiard balls.

The sword of Charlemagne the Just
Is ferric oxide, known as rust.

The grizzly bear whose potent hug
Was feared by all, is now a rug.

Great Caesar's dead and on the shelf,
And I don't feel so well myself!

*Arthur Guiterman*

Der spring is sprung,
Der grass is riz,
I wonder where dem boidies is?

Der little boids is on der wing,
Ain't dat absoid?
Der little wings is on der boid!

The wizard messes up his bench,
Fills the air with smoke and stench.
He seeks the formula for gold,
But all he gets are sludge and mold.

If no one ever marries me—
    And I don't see why they should,
For nurse says I'm not pretty
    And I'm seldom very good—

If no one every marries me
    I shan't mind very much;
I shall buy a squirrel in a cage,
    And a little rabbit hutch.

I shall have a cottage near a wood,
    And a pony all my own,
And a little lamb, quite clean and tame,
    That I can take to town.

And when I'm getting really old,
    At twenty-eight or -nine,
I shall buy a little orphan girl
    And bring her up as mine.

*Laurence Alma-Tadema*

Twinkle, twinkle, little star,
How I wonder what you are!
Up above the world so high,
Like a diamond in the sky.

*Jane Taylor*

## GOLIATH

They chop down 100 ft trees
To make chairs
I bought one
I am six foot one inch.
When I sit in the chair
I'm four foot two.
Did they really chop down a 100 ft tree
To make me look shorter?

*Spike Milligan*

Some talk of Alexander, and some of Hercules;
Of Hector and Lysander, and such great names as these;
But of all the world's brave heroes, there's none that can compare,
With a tow, row, row, row, row, row, for the British Grenadier.

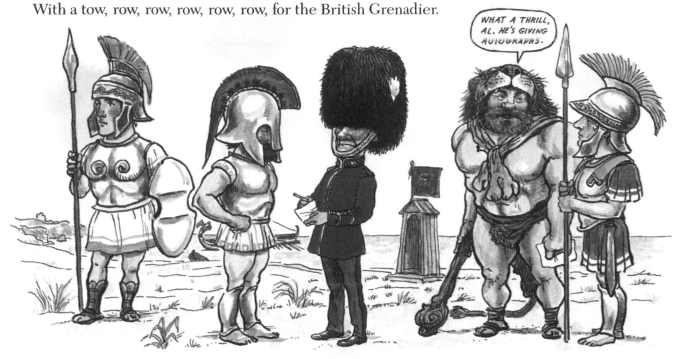

Who are they who rudely jeer
And call the kindly wombat fat?
Why, the hippo, the pig, and other big
Bloated, blubbery twits like that.

*R. Beasley*

I'm nobody! Who are you?
Are you nobody, too?
Then there's a pair of us—don't tell!
They'd banish us, you know.

*Emily Dickinson*

29

I come from the city of Boston,
The home of the bean and the cod,
Where the Cabots speak only to Lowells,
And the Lowells speak only to God.

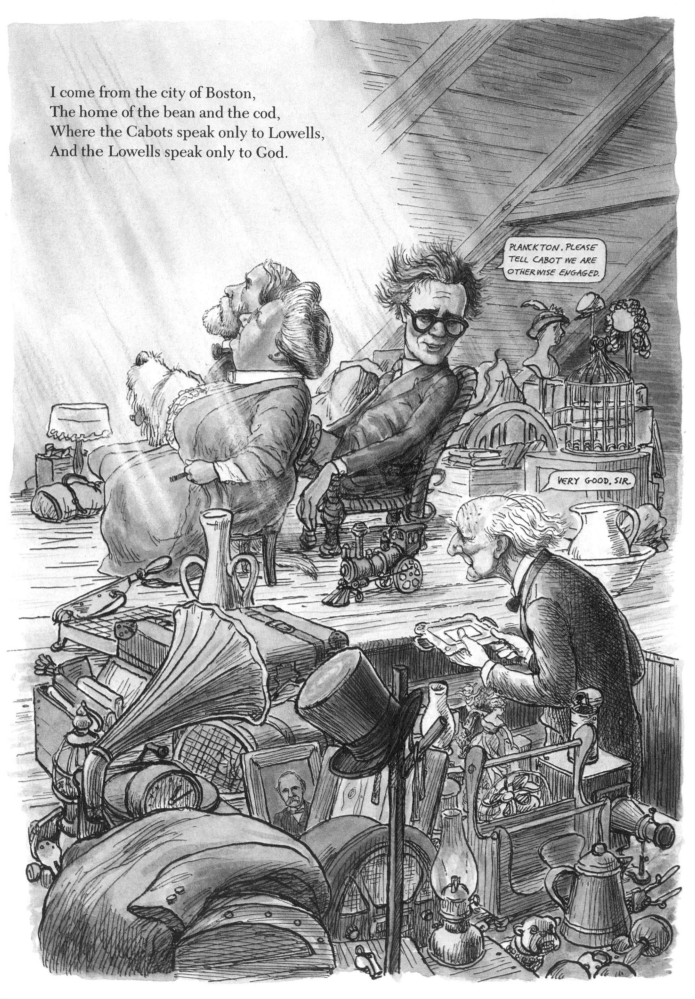

See when a barber and a collier fight,
The barber beats the luckless collier—white;

The dusty collier heaves his ponderous sack,
And big with vengeance beats the barber—black.

In comes the brick-dust man, with grime o'erspread,
And beats the collier and the barber—red:

Black, red, and white in various clouds are tossed,
And in the dust they raise the combatants are lost.

*Christopher Smart*

A strong nor'wester's blowing, Bill!
Hark! don't ye hear it roar now?
Lord help 'em, how I pities them
Unhappy folks on shore now!

*William Pitt*

She said she wasn't hungry,
But this is what she eat:
A dozen raw, a plate of slaw,
A chicken and a roast,
Some applesass, and sparagrass,
And soft-shell crabs on toast.
A big box stew, and crackers too;
Her appetite was immense!
When she called for pie,
I thought I'd die,
For I had but fifty cents.

She said she wasn't thirsty,
Bit this is what she drank:
A gallon pail of ginger ale,
Which made me shake with fear,
A fizzie pop, with foam on top,
A schooner of rootbeer,
A two-quart slug from a cider jug,
She should have had more sense.
When she called for more,
I fell on the floor,
For I had but fifty cents.

When I gave the man the fifty cents,
This is what he done:
He tore my clothes,
He smashed my nose,
He hit me on the jaw,
He gave me a prize
Of a pair of black eyes
And with me swept the floor.
He took me where my pants hung loose,
And threw me over the fence;
Take my advice, don't try it twice
If you've got but fifty cents!

Under a spreading gooseberry bush the village burglar lies,
The burglar is a hairy chap with whiskers round his eyes
And the muscles of his brawny arms keep off the little flies.

He goes on Sunday to the church to hear the parson shout.
He puts a penny in the plate and takes a dollar out
And drops a conscience-stricken tear in case he is found out.

## TEETH

English Teeth, English Teeth!
Shining in the sun
A part of British heritage
Aye, each and every one.

English Teeth, Happy Teeth!
Always having fun
Clamping down on bits of fish
And sausages half done.

English Teeth! HEROES' Teeth!
Hear them click! and clack!
Let's sing a song of praise to them—
Three Cheers for the Brown Grey and Black.

*Spike Milligan*

## REQUEST NUMBER

Tell me a story, Father, please do;
   I've kissed Mama and I've said my prayers,
And I bade good night to the soft pussy cat
   And the little grey mouse that lives under the stairs.

Tell me a story, Father, please do,
   Of power-crazed vampires of monstrous size,
Of hordes of malevolent man-eating crabs
   And pea-green zombies with X-ray eyes.

*G. N. Sprod*

A dog is a pal, so friendly and fun,
The whole darn day he'll bark and run,
And lick you and paw you and fetch and beg,
And, snapping and snuffling, grab your leg.

He'll scratch and he'll sniff and he'll pant and drool,
He'll chomp and nuzzle and act like a fool.

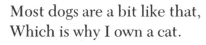

Most dogs are a bit like that,
Which is why I own a cat.

*L. C. Briggs*

Though pleased to see the dolphins play,
I mind my compass and my way.

*Matthew Green*

The giant is great,
The giant is tall,
But the dwarf on his back
Sees farthest of all.

THE GROANING BOARD

A buttery, sugary, syrupy waffle—
Gee, but I love it somep'n awful.
Ginger-cakes dripping with chocolate goo,
Oo! How I love 'em! Oo! *Oo!* OO!

*Pink*

Is that Mr. Riley, can anyone tell?
Is that Mr. Riley that owns the hotel?
Well, if that's Mr. Riley, they speak of so highly,
Upon me soul, Riley, you're doin' quite well.

*Pat Rooney*

I never had a piece of toast
    Particularly long and wide
But fell upon the sanded floor,
    And always on the buttered side.

*James Payn*

I saw a great scholar, apparently thinking,
His brow was knotted, his eyes were blinking.
He chewed on his pencil and wrinkled his nose,
He tapped his fingers and wriggled his toes.
He looked out the window and up at the ceiling,
He sweated and mumbled—but I had the feeling,
That despite outward signs like his ears turning red,
There wasn't a thing going on in his head.

*Maude Crint*

Now I lay me down to sleep,
In mud that's many fathoms deep,
If I'm not here when you awake
Just hunt me with an oyster rake.

As I was laying on the green,
A small English book I seen.
Carlyle's *Essay on Burns* was the edition,
So I left it laying in the same position.

When in danger,
When in doubt,
Run in circles,
Scream and shout.

I am gai, I am poet, I dwell
Rupert Street, at the fifth. I am svell.
    And I sing tralala
    And I love my mamma,
And the English, I speaks him quite well!

*George du Maurier*

There was a young man from the city
Who met what he thought was a kitty.
He gave it a pat
And said, "Nice little cat."
We're sending a wreath out of pity.

The Texan was mighty hungry,
So up to the window he rode.
He was heard to cry,
"Gimme some pie,
And remember the à la mode."

*L. C. Briggs*

My sister she works in a laundry,
My father he fiddles for gin,
My mother she takes in washing.
My gosh, how the money rolls in.

I've scratched the measles, itched the pox,
The mumps they made me drool.
They weren't no fun, not any one—
But they got me out of school!

Early to bed and early to rise
Will make you miss all the regular guys.

*George Ade*

It was a cold and wintry night,
    A man stood in the street;
His aged eyes were full of tears,
    His boots were full of feet.

A Great Dane towers
Over Chihuahuas.

It was John Walker
Who invented the match.
Scritch scritch, scritch scritch,
Scratch, scratch, scratch.

Here's a little proverb that you surely ought to know:
Horses sweat and men perspire, but ladies only glow.

Tommy waved his stick about
And shouted, "Louder, boys!
The English don't like music much
But how they love the noise."

## EPITAPH ON AN UNFORTUNATE ARTIST

He found a formula for drawing comic rabbits:
This formula for drawing comic rabbits paid,
So in the end he could not change the tragic habits
This formula for drawing comic rabbits made.

*Robert Graves*